AWESOME ADVANTAGES
OF BEING A TALL GIRL

AWESOME ADVANTAGES
OF BEING A

TALL GIRL

Patricia Keith-Spiegel, Ph.D.

Library of Congress Control Number: 2019905410

ISBN: 978-0-9971626-9-1

BISAC Codes:
JNF023000 Juvenile Non-Fiction: Girls and Women
JNF024050 Juvenile Non-Fiction: Maturing
JNF053010 Juvenile Non-Fiction: Adolescence

Published by

Big Hat Press
Lafayette, California
www.bighatpress.com

Table of Contents

*Dedicated to a beautiful and
very special tall girl*

Preface

By the fifth grade I was already 5 feet 7 inches tall, the tallest person—boy, girl, or teacher—in the entire elementary school. I was even taller than the male principal! When anyone said "that tall girl" they meant me.

I liked it when teachers put me in charge of group projects and special assignments. I was chosen before many of the boys and all the girls for recess game teams. People seemed to assume that I was smart and strong. I was not sure why.

Only much later did I realize how being taller than the average girl helped shape who I would become as an adult.

But I would be less than candid if I didn't also admit that being vertically noticeable during those pre-teen and teenage years came with snags and disadvantages. I recall adults and some kids asking if I had been held back a year or two because I looked older than my grade level. I recall a mean kid always yelling, "Here comes the giraffe." So annoying.

This book is from my heart for and about girls who are already taller than average or who will likely grow to be at least 5 feet 8 inches tall. It's the book I wish had been available when I was still in school. I would have understood myself and how others saw me so much better.

Acknowledgements

I am so grateful to the many girls and women, most of whom grew to be taller than I, who allowed me to explore the impact of height on their formative years. Their stories offer insights and wisdom about becoming self-fulfilled and confident while managing some challenges related to being vertically different than many others of their age. I give special thanks to three beautiful tall friends, Phyllis Mehan, Janet Roepke, and Peggy Dougherty, who reviewed the entire book prior to its completion.

Thanks also to my editor, Julie Blade, for her keen eye and good ideas and to the incredibly talented Molly Williams at Big Hat Press for putting it all together.

Chat groups, information exchange sites, and blogs provided additional insights and stories from tall girls and boys and their personal search for advice. Especially helpful and noteworthy websites and blogs relevant to tall women are The Tall Society, More Than My Height, and Height Goddess. They reveal how amazing tall girls grow up to be.

Finally, covered in the book are survey and scientific research findings regarding tall people, their prospects in life, and the psychological and the social implications of being tall.

CHAPTER 1

Introduction: Tall Girl Basics

Such a tiny black line. It is one inch long.

The average fully-grown female height is just under 5 feet 4 inches. That adds up to almost 64 tiny black lines end-to-end.

Just a few of those little inches one way or the other wouldn't make any difference to anyone. Right? It turns out that we humans make a big deal out of being taller (and shorter) than average. Only four extra inches puts a girl at 5 feet 8 inches and now defined as tall. Another 4 inches and she's 6 feet.

Approximately 8% of girls born in North America will grow up to be 5 feet 8 inches or taller. They will literally stand above most of their female counterparts, and that makes them instantly noticeable by both girls and boys.

How do others see you? You may be surprised. Some of the unique and extraordinary benefits of being taller than average may not be fully realized until you are a little older.

But before exploring more about being a tall girl, let's look at the full meaning of the word "tall."
It is in the larger context of the meaning of tall that helps make you special in so many positive ways.

CHAPTER 2

In Praise of All Things Tall

What else does tall mean besides height? Tall is exciting. Tall is powerful. Tall means standing above the rest. People are in awe of tallness. The use of the word "tall" almost always implies strength and greatness.

No one cares about the smallest tree, building, waterfall, mountain, or statue. Maybe some people find tiny trees fascinating, such as the dwarf willow at only three inches tall. They are cute, but not awesome. We want to know about the *tallest* things.

The majestic Redwoods (Sequoia sempervirens) are the tallest trees in the world. They can easily reach heights of 300 feet and are found only in northern California.

The tallest building in the world is the stunning Burj Khalifa, built in 2010 and stands at 2,717 feet with 163 floors. It is in Dubai, United Arab Emirates.

Mount Everest, at 29,029 feet, is the tallest mountain above sea level. It is located in the the Himalayas on the border of Nepal and Tibet.

The tallest waterfall in the world is the spectacular Angel Falls (Salto Angel) in Venezuela. The falls are 3,230 feet in height, with an uninterrupted drop of 2,647 feet.

The amazing Statue of Unity was completed in 2018 in the likeness of Sardar Vallabhbhai, the first Prime Minister of independent India. It is the tallest statue at 597 feet.

These five majestic sites are only some of the tall entities that people come from all over the world to admire. Tall is impressive.

CHAPTER 3

The Full Meaning of "Tall" in Everyday Language

What else does tall mean besides height? "Tall" is used in the way we talk every day, almost always to describe strength and admiration. To be associated with tallness is a privilege.

WHAT DOES "LOOK UP TO" MEAN?

When people say, "I look up to...." they are likely describing someone who is honest, good, respected, talented, intelligent, successful, or compassionate, and whose actions exhibit these qualities.

Isn't it interesting that the phrase "look up to" implies tall?

Of course, the point is not to suggest that tall people automatically possess these positive qualities just because of their enhanced height or that shorter people are somehow less worthy. The point is to demonstrate that our language reflects the power and prestige inherent in the concept of tall.

WHAT DOES "STAND TALL" MEAN?

"Stand Tall" is another common and popular term to describe those who are brave, courageous, and willing to defend themselves and others. Those who stand tall care about doing the right thing.

Tall people are more likely to be perceived of as possessing these highly desirable qualities. Their stature suggests leadership skills and confidence. This means you are off to a good start with people who are admiring what kind of a person they perceive you to be.

Remember the power of tall as you read this book. It will help explain many things.

- Why the vast majority of tall adult women are happy with their height.

- Why you get so much attention.

- Why some people are intimidated or even jealous of you.

- Why you are so memorable.

- Why you are viewed as strong and smart.

- Why more may be expected of you.

CHAPTER 4

The Power of Attention

Most people spend a considerable amount of time, money, and effort trying to attract attention to themselves.

It turns out that we humans are born to be showoffs. Some people spend their entire lives—not always successfully—trying to captivate an audience. Some people do dangerous and stupid things just so others will notice them.

Attention, however, is far more important than wanting to be noticed. Unless we are noticed, we do not belong anywhere. And unless we belong to someone or some group, we, as social animals, become depressed and lonely.

What we pay attention to is built into our biological nature. Look at these three illustrations.

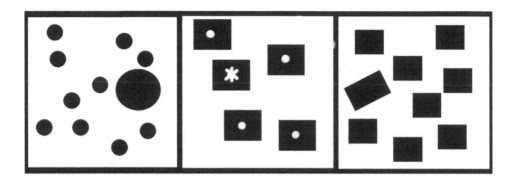

If we hooked you up to a device that tracked your eye movements, yours and everyone else's would look a lot alike. After some bouncing around, the objects attended to most for each of these images would be the largest one, the one that is a little more intriguing, and the one that is a little different.

You can begin to see how being tall fits in here.

So, you don't have to do what most others must do. Without even trying you make an initial impact on others by just being you. Sometimes it may feel like people are staring at you, but more likely than not they are simply admiring your stature.

How do you feel about that?

Do you feel self-conscious and wish you could fade into the walls?

Or, do you use these plentiful opportunities to your advantage?

The key to enjoying positive attention is self-confidence.

Here are some examples of how tall girls and women handled attention.

Andrea finally figured it out.

I used to slouch so people would think I was shorter. That made me look like an old woman. Did I fool anyone? Not a single one! Then one day I just said to myself, "Andrea, stand up straight!" I don't know if it was me or that other people just saw me in a different way, but now I get a lot more respect.

Sara made a common mistake about why people looked at her.

I used to think that everyone looked at me because something was wrong with me. Then one day my friend Lisa said, "It's perfectly natural for others to look at tall people — it's sort of like an involuntary reflex." Instead of trying to be unseen, I use the attention as an opportunity to speak about things I care about. People listen to what I have to say when I stand up proud. Now I can't believe that I used to worry about being tall.

Caroline has a good attitude about her prospects for being tall.

I am probably going to be as tall or taller than my mom, and she is really tall. She is also pretty and lots of fun. So, I am not afraid of the attention I am beginning to get now. People say I am just like she was at my age. Lucky me.

Lily gives others the benefit of the doubt, and that lowers her anxiety.

I notice people looking at me. I guess you could think of it as creepy. Or you could think of it as people just being curious. I think they are interested because I am a little taller than what they are used to seeing in a girl. No foul, no harm. Not a big deal.

Elisabeth conquered a misperception.

I am a little shy, and sometimes I think people see me as arrogant or not interested in them when they ask me questions about my height. I had to work at it, but I am getting more comfortable with people I don't even know coming up to me. They ask the same questions, but I am getting used to them.

Of course, you know that being tall is only one thing about you. The power of attention is that you have a built-in audience to share who else you are. You may not always want or need it, but it holds considerable weight when you have a point to make or something to share.

CHAPTER 5

Being Unforgettable

"No one remembers me." What a sad way for anyone to feel!

You have heard that elephants have superior memories. It's true. They do.

Fortunately, you, as a taller girl, will not experience that sorrowful feeling of not being remembered.

You do not blend into a faceless, nameless crowd. When you enter a room, you have already made your first impression. Tallness is a distinctive characteristic that aids memory. In a sense, people are like elephants when it comes to you! They remember who you are.

Neuroscience research tells us that attention and remembering go together. The brain activity cements the source of attention into memories. You are a source of attention, and that turns into a memory of you.

Denise doesn't have the same problem as her friends who are shorter.

My friends complain that they run into someone familiar, and then that person says something like, "Who are you again?" That rarely happens to me. People may not recall my full name, but they remember me, where we met, and what we talked about. I stick!

Being easily remembered will be helpful to you in a great many ways, now and for your whole life. Barbara's story is a common theme.

I interviewed for a fantastic summer internship at a radio station. I thought I didn't have a chance, but I got the job. My boss later told me that he conducted almost fifty interviews, but his clearest memory was of me. He joked that it was because I was tall, but I believe my height really did help me.

Rachel faces a problem with being so memorable. She needs to improve her own memory!

It can be so embarrassing. People remember me, but I often draw a blank as to who they are or how I came to know them. I worry that they think I am a snob or saw them as not important enough to remember. I don't like to hurt people's feelings.

Deanne meets more people.

It's so much easier to get to know people when you are taller. Once introduced they always remember me, even after months have passed. I am good with names and faces so I remember them as well. It's fun to have so many friends.

Maybe you do not always want people to walk away with total recall about you. There is not a lot you can do about that. But you can consider the words of the famous poet Maya Angelou who said, *"I've learned that people will forget what you said, people will forget what you did, but people will never forget how you made them feel."* Allow others to see the capable, good person you want them to know and remember.

CHAPTER 6

You Look Great in Clothes

Women dress to be noticed. Some go way out — sometimes too far — to make sure everyone takes a good look.

Tall girls have not-always appreciated this advantage because it happens automatically. You can wear plain and simple styles and still be admired because you look good in just about any outfit!

Most of the top professional fashion models are between 5 feet 9 inches to 6 feet one inches. Some are even taller. According to the Guinness World Records, the tallest professional model in the world is the gorgeous Ekaterina Lisina. She is almost 6 feet 9 inches.

It wasn't that long ago that a girl taller than 5 feet 9 inches could not find clothes that fit her properly. The waist rode up high on her rib cage. Pants hit her well above the ankle, even though that look was not in style. Skirts were usually too short, even when mini-

skirts were "in." Short dresses were more like tunics or long shirts. Crop tops were more like underwear. Long sleeves were three-quarter sleeves. Such misfits existed because manufacturers created clothing for the 5-foot 4 inch woman and then expanded the same proportions up for larger sizes. They figured if you go up you also go out. No account was taken for the longer legs, arms, and torsos compared to the average proportioned female.

If you bought a large size, it was often too wide. Most tall girls tend to be on the slim side during their early teenage years.

The taller you are the more challenging it is to explore available options, especially for pants if your legs are very long. (Shorter girls often complain that the pants curl up around their ankles and that the fashionable long shirt styles make them look like tubes with feet.)

Happily, things have changed in your favor. You may spend more time buying off-the-rack because it is still hit-and-miss for tall girls. But you won't always come up empty because many stores now have a "tall line."

Online shopping options are now plentiful, offering every type of garment and accessory created for the tall body. Even tall size pajamas! The downside here is that you cannot try them on first. Check the return policies before buying.

Here are some helpful shopping tips offered by tall girls and women:

Beware! If the neck is low, lean forward to see what others can see before you buy. You will be bending to talk to or hug shorter people, so you don't want to show off what you don't want share!

Tall clothes still tend to be basic, fashion-neutral styles. If you want to glam up, add additional interest to your outfit. Think scarves, costume jewelry, pins, wraps, and the like.

Caution! "One-size-fits-all" usually does not include you! I learned this the hard way. I saw an outfit I loved and thought I could just alter it. But you usually cannot lengthen the sleeves or hems because there is not enough fabric to work with.

Because skirts and dresses look much shorter on me, I have been accused of trying to be sexy when that was absolutely not my intent.

Encourage local stores and boutiques to

carry more items made for taller girls and women. They want your business, so they will listen.

But back to the main point. *TALL GIRLS LOOK GREAT WEARING ALMOST ANYTHING!* Wow! What an incredible advantage in a society that places a considerable emphasis on how good we look in public. Having a long, statuesque appearance is always admired whether it be in an evening gown or casual daywear. You don't have to be flashing with bling or wild colors unless you want to.

So, wear what you like and enjoy looking marvelous!

CHAPTER 7

Oh, Those Legs!

So where does tall come from?

Much of it from longer limbs. Long legs are highly valued and admired. (Just ask any shorter person!)

Surveys reveal that men are not alone in rating women with longer legs as more appealing. Women also find longer women's legs to be more attractive.

Terra remembers how her legs changed.

When I was thirteen I had very long legs, but they were skinny and straight. A boy down the street enjoyed calling me "Toothpick" and "Q-Tip." I always turned red, and he thought that was even funnier. By age fourteen my legs began to get a shape. When I was fifteen that same boy asked me to go to a party with him. I enjoyed turning him down.

Fashion models don't get to be successful because they are wafer-thin and sport grumpy expressions while promenading down a runway. It's those long

legs that make them special. Another reason most fashion models are tall is because their height is associated with dignity and prestige. A taller stature creates a profound presence on the runway. What they are wearing also gets attention, and that is every designer's goal.

Finally, we go to to Gina's cousin's wedding. Gina looks great. The others? Not so much.

When I was seventeen my cousin asked me to be in her wedding party. There were four bridesmaids, and I was by far the thinnest and tallest at 6 feet. The other bridesmaids were around 5 feet 2 inches tall. The dresses my cousin chose were moss green and draped in many layers almost to the floor. The top was tight and straight. Laura, one of the other bridesmaids, whispered just as we were getting ready to walk down the aisle,

"*Gina looks terrific, but the rest of us look like artichokes turned upside down!*" *We had to stifle our giggles during the whole ceremony.*

The graceful and elegant vision of a long-legged woman is unique. Long legs cannot be faked. You either have them or you don't. You do!

CHAPTER 8

You Don't Have to Wear High Heels (Unless You Want to)

It can be difficult for girls with larger feet to find shoes that fit properly. Your tall mother probably could not say to the shoe store salesperson, "Please bring out a size 10 version

of this cute little size 4 on display." Instead, she had to ask, "Do you have *anything at all* in size 10?" If she was lucky, the salesperson said *"yes."* But the few pairs he brought out probably had little to do with what she was looking for.

Ruth recalls those older days well.

My tall daughter has it so much better than I did. Most of the size 10 shoes I could find when I was a girl were strange looking and could double as a couple of steamboats for my Barbie dolls.

Fortunately, things have changed. You may not always have a large selection compared to smaller shoe sizes, but you usually don't have to worry about ending up with nothing that fits. Today, finding stylish shoes up to size 11 is easy. A few places (including online shops) cater to women with shoe sizes up to 15.

Some tall women like to add two or three additional inches to their already statuesque figures. For some outfits, high heels do look striking. Shorter women wear them to make their legs appear to be longer and to look taller. (In fact, many surveys reveal that most shorter women wish they were taller!)

You already have great legs and you are already taller. So here is good news about tall women and high heels. You will never *have* to wear them unless you really want to. This is more of a blessing than you may realize.

High heels are dangerous and often uncomfortable. The higher the heel the more unstable you are. Falling or getting those heels stuck in cracks are common unfortunate events. Your shoe is ruined, and you could even break an ankle. Pray you never have a reason to run!

High heels can do severe damage to your feet and tendons if worn frequently. Those unsightly lumps are called bunions. They hurt. Painful corns and knee discomfort are caused by gravity forcing your feet to smash up against the toe end of the shoe.

Destiny learned the hard way.

Now at age 37 my feet are killing me most of the time. I have no choice but to buy special shoes, and they are so ugly. If I had worn flat shoes more often, I wouldn't need surgery.

You may now be saying to yourself, "But I *want* to wear high heels—at least sometimes." Here are some hints from experts:

- Never, ever buy shoes a size or two smaller to make your feet look smaller. Your feet will soon hate you.

- If you have never worn heels before, start out with short ones (one or one-and-a half inches) and wear them for only an hour or so at a time. Practice before venturing out.

- Buy styles that feel comfortable and safe. Some styles help you remain steadier than others.

- If anyone makes a snide comment such as, "Why do you want to look even taller than you already are?" consider responding with something like, "I dress to please myself." (And then smile.)

What about flat shoes? Not counting a huge selection of boots, sandals, athletic shoes and sneakers in larger sizes, flat shoes now come in hundreds of styles and colors. The array of designs is dazzling, from formal black to rainbow with glitter. And they don't look like steamboats!

Brenda finds value in comfortable shoes!

My best friend at work is just over 5 feet tall. She believes she needs to wear three-inch heels to be taken seriously. Her feet often hurt, and it shows on her face. She looks like she just swallowed a big bug. She envies me because I am 5 feet, 10 inches and can wear flat shoes and remain visible. I know that feeling comfortable on the job helps to keep me in a good mood. I can also accomplish more, and the boss takes notice.

The average person should walk 8,000 steps a day to stay healthy. Our feet, no matter how tall we are, deserve the best care. That means comfort, support, and the right size. We can't take our feet for granted.

CHAPTER 9

Teenagers' Obsession with Dieting – Probably Not Your Problem!

For better or for worse, THIN IS IN. When it comes to the visual image that girls and women want everyone to admire, a slender shape rises to the top

of the list. Hair, skin, eyes, clothes, and anything else people can see is of lesser importance.

According to the US National Institutes of Health, about half of all teenage girls attempt to diet, even though a substantial number of them are at a healthy weight.

You see skinny everywhere. Movies, television, advertisements, friends, and sometimes parents constantly push a slim shape as a primary personal goal for how teens and young women should look. Weight loss products and diet books fly off the shelves. New fads promising to take the pounds off fast are big business.

Even a few extra pounds are to be shaved off as soon as possible using anything that works. Skipping meals, vomiting after eating, laxatives, and crash diets may work for a while but at the expense of physical health and emotional wellbeing. Losing weight can become an obsession. A percentage of teenage dieters will end up with eating disorders that, in more serious cases, can be life-threatening.

The sad news is that most diets do not work, partially because it is difficult to commit to a strict eating program when greasy fast food and sweets are so readily available.

Now here is the great news for you. You, as a tall girl, are probably on the slender side and can eat whatever you want (for now, anyway) because you went more *up* than *out*. An extra few pounds won't even show. Any teen struggling to control her weight is so jealous of you! Of course, tall girls eventually grow up to be stunning women in a variety of shapes and sizes.

Those Annoying Questions Are (Usually) Compliments

If you are already tall, you are probably used to getting "tall" questions, even from strangers. If not, be prepared!

Do you play basketball?

Do you want to be a model?

How's the weather up there?

Can you reach that for me?

How long were you when you were born?

Do you have to duck a lot?

Do you have trouble buying clothes?

How tall are you?

What is your shoe size?

Are your parents tall?

Will you get taller?"

Do you realize how short you make me feel?

Sometimes people inform you that you are tall, as if you hadn't already noticed!

It is curious that people seem to feel secure in approaching tall people to ask about or comment on their height. Questioning people about their weight, shortness, nose shape, skin color, or other bodily feature would usually be seen as intrusive and even rude. So, why is openly questioning tall people about their height so socially acceptable? Only one reason makes sense. They assume that you are proud of being tall and not the least bit sensitive about it. The message is, "I see who you are, and you are impressive."

Curious people do not intend to be upsetting or disrespectful. They just want to interact with you. This is not to say that the questions and comments don't feel stale after a while.

Chloe holds it together.

When someone says, "You are really tall" I want to snort, "Oh, thank you so much for letting me know." But I think their mouth is just reflecting what they see, so I usually respond with something like, "Yes, I am very lucky."

The questions can also be motivated by wanting to convey something nice about you.

Jasmine just changes the subject.

When someone says, "You should be a model" I take that as a compliment. I just say, "Thanks" and move on to another topic.

Sierra gives people a pass.

When I am asked if my parents are tall or how long I was when I was born, I know they aren't trying to be too personal. They are just curious and assume I'm fine with my height.

Sometimes the questions give you an opportunity to convey something about yourself. Makayla turns the conversation around and keeps it going.

People think every tall girl wants to be a model. When people ask me, I politely say, "No, I want to be a dentist" because that is what I do want to be. Then we might talk about dental hygiene.

People like to tease, and they may not realize that a quip about height can come across as insensitive. They are trying to be amusing, even if it doesn't strike you that way.

Megan puts up with it.

I hate that weather-up-there question. I am only 1 inch taller than the last guy who asked me that. He needs a new line.

Sometimes the questions can feel inappropriately intrusive. Again, the person may be curious because your stature alone makes you an "interesting individual."

Mary is ready with her responses.

I admit that I feel uncomfortable when someone asks me about how tall the guys are that I date. My response is always something like, "It doesn't matter how tall people are. I have dated guys shorter and taller than I am. I care about who they are on the inside." Sometimes I give examples of

*famous couples where the man is shorter, like George Cloo-
ney and his wife Amal Alamuddin or Nicole Kidman and
Keith Urban, and before Keith, Tom Cruise.*

You may also be saying to yourself that people are
not always motivated by curiosity or good intentions.
You are correct. You may be tempted to respond in
kind. Here are a couple of examples (not recommended here) floating around the Internet.

*When people ask me if I play basketball, I say, "No, do you
play miniature golf?"*

*Once someone asked, "Do you get nose bleeds in that rari-
fied atmosphere?" I said, "No, it's clean and fresh. How are
you surviving way down there in that toxic smog?"*

Pick your battles. Not all are
worth fighting. This isn't to
say that you should endure
questions you are certain
were meant to cause you
embarrassment or emotional
pain. Use your tall power to
inform the person that what
they are asking is unaccept-
able. It's always wise to seek
assistance from your parents
or school staff if you need it.

But do remember that the people making comments and asking questions likely mean no disrespect. You are noticed, and far more than likely in a good way.

CHAPTER 11

The Sporting Edge

Wonder Woman is the most popular female superhero of all time. She first appeared in a DC comic book almost 80 years ago. And, she is tall!

The fictional Wonder Woman character is an Amazon princess who stands at 6 feet. She is strong and athletic. She is a courageous warrior who fearlessly defends those who need help.

People perceive tall girls as strong and athletic. And many do excel (or can if they want to) in those sports that would be challenging for girls of average height.

Basketball is always the first game that comes to mind. How tall was the average female player on the US Olympics team in 2016? About 6 feet one inch. How many Olympic gold medals has the US women's team won? Eight altogether, including six in the last consecutive six games!

Are there sports besides basketball that give tall girls the sporting edge? Yes, several. Long legs rule in sprinting. For tall girls who are agile, height is a plus in table tennis, badminton, and fencing.

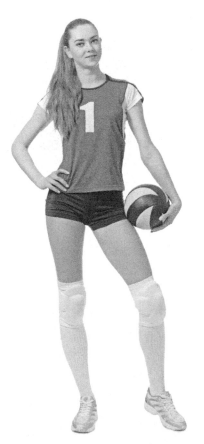

Volleyball requires height to serve and slam with a deft torque and to create a formidable block. Shorter volley ball players can fulfill backrow defense roles but being tall is definitely an advantage in volleyball. Kerri Walsh Jennings, the popular three-time Olympic gold medalists in beach volley, stands at 6 feet 3 inches.

For tall girls with more muscle mass and a medium body type, add in the javelin, swimming, shotput, and martial arts. And rowing should not be overlooked. Tall girls can stroke a wide expanse of water.

Some tall girls fear that they will be seen as masculine if they go out for sports. At one time an apprehension of being perceived as a "tomboy" kept girls away from anything boys did. But the "ideal woman image" has made huge shifts in recent years, from being tiny and dainty to a "can do" gal who keeps up with the action. In today's movies and TV shows women rarely cower in the corner when the going gets tough. Instead they jump right in. So, even if sports do not appeal that much to you now, or if you think you would not be very good at them, at least consider the stories told by girls who were also skeptical at first:

Bobbi gets a boost from a friend.

I felt so klutzy as a fourteen-year-old. I would even trip over my own big feet. The thought of doing anything requiring me to look graceful made me sputter. Then a guy nagged me to try swimming. Good call! I am not the best member of my team, but I feel like a ballerina in the water.

Yvonne put running to good use.

Little did I know that running lightning fast was more than just something I could do. One day a high school coach

happened to see me galloping across the field to get to class. Later he asked me to join our girl's track and field team. Boom! I kept at it and became the top sprinter in college.

Tennis didn't cut it, but basketball worked out great for Ida.

I felt clumsy as I was growing taller and taller. My parents encouraged me to try tennis. I kept stumbling when moving sideways, but I did like being on a court. So,

I switched to basketball. I practiced and became a pretty good player. But, here's the honest truth. It wasn't about basketball at all. It was about being on a team with other super girls, having fun, and sharing our lives. I belonged to something bigger than myself.

Belinda found that her long, flexible body meant that gymnastics was in her future. She is just starting, but things look promising.

When I was a little kid, I liked doing summersaults and cartwheels on the back-yard grass. Now I am working my way up to more challenging moves and have signed up for a gymnastics class.

Marlene, Casey, and Thelma were always open to sports, and it made a positive difference in their lives.

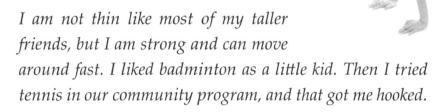

My mom said, "Find a passion and follow it." It was volleyball. I was the tallest girl on the team, so I was able to slam and block when most of my team mates couldn't. I was the star.

I am not thin like most of my taller friends, but I am strong and can move around fast. I liked badminton as a little kid. Then I tried tennis in our community program, and that got me hooked.

My grandma thought that girls exceeding in sports was "not ladylike." I had to explain to her that a lot has changed. Women's sports have become popular, and girls who participate are admired. I also told her about how good sports made me feel about my body and who I am. She gave me a kiss and said, "I guess I am way behind the times. Good for you, Thelma."

Many of the most outstanding female athletes are also tall and among the most beautiful women in the world. Here are some examples (including their sports and heights):

Michelle Wie 6'1" Golf

Maria Sharapova 6'2" Tennis

Jenny Finch 6' Softball

Kerri Walsh Jennings 6'3"
Beach Volleyball

Amy Acuff 6'2" High Jump

Yvetta Hlavacova 6'4" Swimming

Elena Delle Donne 6'5" Basketball

Gabrielle Reece 6'3" Volleyball

Venus Williams 6'1" Tennis

Candace Parker 6'4" Basketball

Missy Franklin 6'2" Swimming

Blanka Vlašić 6'3" High Jump

The women interviewed for this book often enthusi-astically suggested that participation in a sport that is right for you could be a pathway to self-confidence, friendships, and admiration by others. Something to think about seriously.

CHAPTER 12

Tall and Smart

Intelligent people are highly valued and admired. Universities and employers want them. Maybe that "really smart kid" in school—there is always at least one—is enduring some teasing now, but she or he will have the last laugh later.

Here is a fascinating research-based fact. Tall people are almost *automatically perceived* to be smart. Unlike everyone else, you don't have to do anything to prove it. You are an impressive sight, so people think you must also be smart (unless, of course, you prove otherwise).

But wait!

Many scientific studies report a relationship between height and intelligence. Maybe tall people have inherited "smart genes." One large study concluded that tall children's superior cognitive abilities show up as early as age three, before any schooling effect has a chance to take place.

Because teachers may perceive taller students as more capable, they may be more encouraging and demanding, resulting in better performances on intellectual tasks.

Katelyn figured that out early.

Even in elementary school our teachers zoomed in on the tall kids, both the boys and girls. They chose us more often to carry out special assignments, including helping teach the slower kids. They seemed to think that we were more capable of handling tasks requiring responsibility. But here is my little secret. Their trust is what taught me to be responsible, not the other way around!

It could also be that tall parents who often have better jobs (as discussed in the next chapter) were able to provide a more enriched environment, outside learning aids such as private tutors, and better nutrition for their tall children.

Eye contact may also be a factor in perceiving tall people as smarter. Others have no choice but to glance upwards to see eye-to-eye with a tall person. The tall person must look down to maintain eye contact with anyone shorter than they are. A dynamic is set that sends an unconscious (and not usually intended) message from the taller person; "I am bigger and smarter than you are."

Of course, not all tall people are smart, and people of average or shorter height can be just as brilliant as the smartest tall person. After all, Albert Einstein was only 5 feet 8 inches tall, which is an inch shorter than today's average-sized man. But the combination of perceptions by others of tall people's intelligence along with the correlational studies suggesting that, on average, taller people score somewhat higher cognitive tests can open many types of doors in a society that richly rewards high intellect.

CHAPTER 13

Tall On the Job

Chances are high that you will be employed for a good part of your adult life. About 75% of women have been. Does your height have anything to do with your future career? Yes, it turns out it does.

A height bias exists in the workplace, and it clearly favors tall people. It has been called the "Height Premium." This means that when you enter the job market, your chances of landing a good position are greater just because you are taller. Why?

We've known for a long time that taller men, overall, are more successful career-wise than shorter men. Here are some amazing statistics. In the U.S. population, about 14.5% of all men are 6 feet tall or taller. However, 58% of the heads of Fortune 500 companies are over 6 feet tall!

What about taller women? It turns out that this trend is heading upwards for them as well. Barriers that once divided jobs and careers into gender-based stereotypes have shattered. Women can now be surgeons,  fork-lift operators, firefighters, truck drivers, astronauts, jet pilots, sportscasters, heads of small and large companies, and FBI agents, to name a few. To the extent that taller humans are seen as stronger and more dominant, you can aspire to be whatever you prepare yourself to be.

Employers favor taller people even in non-professional and middle-level jobs, especially sales and managerial positions. Fair or not, there appears to be an assumption that tallness is a sign to employers of worker quality in both male and female applicants.

Tall men and women also earn more money. Recent surveys found that women 5 feet 8 inches and taller earned annual salaries averaging $6,500 more than shorter women do.

Here is how Robin sees her success.

My 5-foot 9 inch mother told me more times than I could ever count that much would be expected of me because I was going to be tall. I was worried, wondering if I could keep up with how others saw me. She convinced me to study hard so that I would be ready for everything that came my way. She was right. As I grew, strangers thought I was three grades higher than I was and expected me to carry on conversations about current events and other subjects that my same-age friends were not really into. I learned early on to act more like an adult around adults because I was being treated like one. That helped me at least appear to be more mature, and I think that is one reason why I did so much better in school than most of my classmates. Teachers even told me that they liked my "grown-up behavior." So, what did I grow up to be? I am now a doctor specializing in treating childhood diseases.

The ability to be a leader is related to successful careers and visibility in one's social and local community. Tall men and women are automatically perceived as having leadership skills. It may be part of our evolutionary path to view the largest and more imposing-looking of the species as being more assertive, of possessing more dominant skills, as having greater intelligence, and as able to take more risks. It should be no surprise, then, that so many tall people are "in charge."

Mila can have any community leadership position she wants.

It's a family joke. Anytime someone or a group is looking for an organizer, I get the call. It almost doesn't matter what the need is. It can be a book club meeting, an after-school event, a class Halloween party, a celebration for an out-of-town dignitary, or a city commission opportunity. I am convinced it's because I have always enjoyed being 6 feet tall. But people read far more into it than that. They think I can do anything.

Twila hated being tall until she saw the benefits of the attention that helped fulfill her own leadership goals.

When I was thirteen and already 5 feet 8 inches tall, I prayed I would never get taller. I was teased about being as tall or taller than many of the boys, and I thought something went whacky with my genes because neither parent is as tall as I am. I dreamed of being a student leader, but that seemed out of the question. Little did I know then that my height, now 5 feet 11 inches, would be a path to my success. In college I began to see the immediate attention was something I could work with. It was like having an on-call stage and microphone. That made it easy to talk to people about my ideas. Now in my senior year I am class president.

Here's an important point to make again. The tall advantage in the workplace is strongly related to

self-confidence. Women who try to minimize their stature by slouching will fail to reap the rewards of their height. Instead, they come off as nervous, withdrawn, and insecure. This is not an image that attracts employers (or anyone else).

So always stand tall and have the confidence that your height will benefit you in ways you may not yet fully realize. You will likely have a job during a substantial period of your life. It doesn't hurt to begin to think now about careers that interest you and what effort you need to put forth to get there. Being tall will help get in the door, but then you must prove you can do the job.

CHAPTER 14

Unkind Jokes – Tall People Don't Have It as Bad

Everyone loves a good laugh. Laughter boosts the body's energy. Laughter reduces stress. Laughter is relaxing and improves our moods. We like to be with people who make us laugh.

In a perfect world all humor would be amusing. No one would feel put down or marginalized.

But humor and laughter have their dark sides. A gap exists between "laughing with" and "laughing at." Jokes are often insulting when the target is a member of an identifiable group.

As a tall girl you may be present when someone tells a joke about tall people. But here's the thing: There aren't very many of them, and those that do exist are just plain stupid and corny. Some reflect a thinly-veiled jealousy of your advantaged stature.

For most tall jokes, height is simply exaggerated which, in a way, makes the tall targets bigger than life. Not really all that bad! Here are a few of examples:

Where did the tall girl find a boyfriend? At the top of a step ladder

What does a tall person do when they see an airplane coming? Duck.

What do clowns and tall people have in common? Their shoe stores.

It's not tall people's fault they think they're the center of the universe. They just can't see anyone else.

What's a tall person's worst fear? Ceiling fans.

How do you make tall people angry? Pick them up in a small car.

How do you react?

Before deciding your response, it's insightful to realize that jokes about short people are far more prevalent and tend to be more insulting and demeaning, often downright cruel. Here are a few of the milder examples:

You're so short you could bungee jump off a curb.

You're so short that if you pulled up your socks you'd be blind.

You're so short that you can't tell whether you have a head-ache or sore feet.

You can empathize with how stupid these short people jokes are.

How you respond to those who tell jokes also depends on who told it, where it was told, and how it made you feel in the moment. There is no single correct way to react to a tall joke. If you thought the joke was funny, just laugh with whoever is telling it. Sometimes target jokes are clever and even flattering. Tall people tell other tall people jokes to each other, creating an in-group comradery. A shorter friend may be trying to have some innocent fun by texting you a tall joke, but you can tell him or her if it bothers you. If you thought the joke was unkind or insulting and crossed your line, let the joke-teller know. The person will think twice before telling it again. Be prepared to hear, "Oh, I was just kidding."

Tall and short jokes refer to *all* tall and *all* short people. They are not directed specifically at any individual, including you. Teasing and bullying are something else again. This time it's personal. It's directed at you, although, as revealed in Chapter 17, it isn't really about you at all.

CHAPTER 15

Finding Each Other

There is truth in the old saying, "Birds of a feather flock together." That includes tall people being attracted to each other, at least for friendship and support. You have a lot in common and issues to discuss.

Most people searching for sidekicks who share the same interests must do some serious digging. How do you go about locating people who want to learn how to shoot a bow and arrow, go fishing, find play dates for their dogs at the park, enjoy a certain videogame, or collect action figures or vintage toy cars? It will probably take time to ask around before you gather up a soul mate. You may have to settle for virtual like-minded individuals online.

If you want some tall friends, all you need to do is look around. They will reveal themselves without doing any research or asking any questions.

Audrey had a plan.

When I started high school, I noticed three girls as tall as I am and one who was even taller. I just went up to each one to introduce myself. Then I said I wanted to know what to expect. I asked them how they were treated. They were all nice to me and mostly put my mind at ease. Two of them became my good friends.

Zena found a guy.

When you are in a group you can see the taller heads pop up over the rest. Sometimes we smile or wave, even though we don't know each other. I met a guy that way. He waved, I waved back. We were at the snack stand at a football game, so we sat next to each other for second half. After that we dated until his family had to move out of town.

Of course, being tall is hardly your only focus in life, and you don't need only tall friends. But it is both satisfying and enlightening to know a few people who also stand tall. They can be of any age. You can probably count on them to understand any issues you may be facing. And, you can help them if they need some support.

CHAPTER 16

Four Great Perks: Running, Reaching, Standing Above the Crowd, and the Passenger Seat

Your tall body and long limbs have advantages that can make your day-to-day life easier and much safer. You can run faster. You can reach higher. And you can find your way around much better in crowds. And then there's that front car seat. Others envy all these advantages!

FAST ON YOUR FEET

That long gait means that physically active tall girls can move faster than shorter people. The advantage of long legs is not confined to track and field sports. The ability to take off and run can come in handy. You can catch a bus, get to where you need to be on time, or get out of the way much faster than most shorter people.

Jane's dog has a best friend.

My dog Sanchez lives for his 4 p.m. long walk. It's like he has a built-in clock. But he wants to run. Our city ordinance requires dogs to always be on a leash. I am the only one in my family who can almost keep up with him.

Friends grumble about Nancy.

My friends who are shorter than I am always complain when we walk together that I am too fast. I'm usually not taking any more steps than they are, mine are just longer. I laugh and tell them that keeping up with me is a great exercise for them.

Being quick on your feet can even be lifesaving. Nella is grateful for Kay, her teenage neighbor who is 6-feet one inch tall.

I'm 5 feet even and a little out of shape. Last month my three-year-old child got out of the yard and started racing down the middle of the street on his scooter. Despite running as fast as I could, I wasn't able to catch up. If Kay hadn't taken notice and raced on by me to grab him, I don't even want to think about what might have happened.

REACHING

Being able to put up or get to things on high shelves may not seem like a big deal if you are already tall.

But every person of average or shorter height envies those who can retrieve items that are beyond their reach. Most people must keep a stepladder handy and hope they don't topple off when they have no choice but to use it, which is often.

Gretta puts up with the requests.

Sometimes I get a little annoyed if I am busy doing my own thing and a family member demands that I come right away to reach for something high in the garage. If I called them to pick something up off the floor, would they do it? Anyway, I am grateful for my ability to reach because I use it all the time for myself.

Kenzie gets compliments in the market.

It is common for strangers to come up and tell me how lucky I am to be able to get food off the high shelf without having to call a clerk for help. I admit it does make shopping much easier. Once I saw a woman trying to get a big bag of rice off the top shelf and it crashed down on her head. Rice flew everywhere. She was so embarrassed. So now I feel good when I help those I see struggling to reach up high. I know I could be saving them from the same kind of trouble.

STANDING ABOVE THE CROWDS

Young people spend quite a bit of their time in crowds: Sport events, concerts, dances, malls, school hallways and grounds, and parties. Any time a large group occupies the same space, tall people have a much better view. They can see better and further. Their friends can find them easily.

Marlene is comfortable at concerts.

Outdoor rock concerts and music festivals are the pits for people who are not tall. Everyone stands through the whole performance, and unless you are in the front few rows or up on a hill—if there is a hill—you only get to hear it. As for me, I can see everything no matter where I end up unless I am behind someone taller than me.

Joan's friends like her height.

My friends appreciate me whenever we decide to meet up. They say, "Just look for Joan!"

Abigale has it made at parades.

We go to the Rose Parade in Pasadena, California almost every year and stand along the curb. Several rows of people always get there before we do. I feel bad for most of them who need to get up on their tiptoes for a glance at the tops of the floats. I can easily see every flower on every float almost from the ground up.

Trying to find shorter friends in a crowd is almost impossible unless they are wearing a top hat or have a balloon. Most people of average height or shorter will have a harrowing incident to share about trouble linking up with friends or getting swallowed up in a crowd.

THE PASSENGER SEAT

Finally, if someone else is driving others and you are the tallest of the others, you will be offered the passenger seat 99% of the time. No sharing with little kids or scrunching your legs into the back seat. You can enjoy looking out the window with the best view and enjoy that extra leg room!

CHAPTER 17

Looking Down on Teasers and Bullies (and What Else You Need to Know About Them)

Anyone can fall victim to mean-spirted teenagers. Tall girls are no exception. The goal for this chapter is to frame how unkind words and actions can often be interpreted in another way that will change how you see a tormenter.

Fortunately, tall girls have leverage against teasers and bullies that other target groups do not. So, let's start with the advantages you have with-face-to-face verbal assaults.

- First, no one who is as tall or taller than you is likely to tease or bully you about being tall.

- All else being equal, it is probably more difficult to tease or bully someone when he or she must (literally!) look *up* to see their target. From a psychological perspective, those who harass tall people are already in a one-down position.

- Tall people are larger and perhaps stronger than same-aged teens. Bullies may be concerned that a taller teen might be upset enough to fight—and win! So, stand up as straight as you can and look down at bullies. That alone sends a message.

It's important to note that bullying tall girls and tall boys is less common overall. Teens are more likely to be harassed about their weight, race, facial or other bodily features, sexual orientation, clothes, intellectual capabilities, social status, and very short stature.

Sadly, everyone has been teased or bullied at least a few times while growing up. Here is a list gathered from friends—both young and old—recalling some nasty comments they endured as teens.

Teeth shape: *You look like a vampire.*

Hair style: *Have you ever heard of a comb?*

Weight: *Do you wear size tent?*

Eyes: *How can you see out of those tiny holes?*

Clothes: *You must shop exclusively at Goodwill.*

Body parts: *Have you ever thought of chopping off some of that huge nose?*

Intelligence: *You are too dumb to be in school.*

Social status: *You're not one of us and never will be.*

Physical disability: *You walk like a lizard.*

A family member: *How can you be seen with such an ugly sister?*

Just plain mean: *I am having a party, but you are not invited.*

Bullies and teasers sometimes call people unkind and unflattering names. A short person may be referred to as mini-me, firecracker, shrimp, shortcake, bite-size, tater tot, squirt, ankle biter, or goober, to name just a few. A tall person may be called Amazon, giant-ess, tower, string bean, giraffe, stretch, stilts, big foot, or (paradoxically) tiny or shorty. It can be annoying when one of those names sticks.

Julia and her best friend got saddled with names all through high school.

My best friend Enid was only 5 feet tall, and I was almost 6 feet by the ninth grade. Someone stated calling us String Bean and Little Sprout. It caught on fast. At first we were upset, but soon it became kind of a badge of honor. We just didn't let it bother us.

Ruth, Ginny, and Ally tell their individual stories. Notice how all three girls stood up and responded in a way that minimized their own embarrassment.

When I was called "Amazon" I replied, "Thank you. Those women were strong and superior. I appreciate the compli-ment." They never called me that again.

My best friend called me Skinny Ginny. She was on a diet, so I said, "Did you know those weight loss products are a multibillion dollar a year industry? I am lucky enough to not have to buy any of them." She smiled and never used that name again.

When some boys yelled, "Hey Lamp Post," I said, "Do you enjoy hurting people's feelings? Is that how you have fun?"

They looked taken aback and turned away. One of them even came up later and said, "Sorry I was part of that Ally."

So, if you are teased in an obnoxious or vulgar way about being tall, your height is just the feature the nasty person picked out about you. Some of your classmates are being teased just as frequently (probably more).

Now to mean teasers and bullies themselves. Who are they? Once you know more about them, you may even feel a little bit sorry for these unhappy, insecure individuals.

Why do they do it? There are two basic types of bullies. One kind needs to retain the power they have (or think they have) by putting other people down. The other types are kids who are isolated from their peers, have low self-esteem and emotional problems, or are unable to empathize with the feelings of others. For both types, hurting others' feelings makes them feel better about themselves. Social media bullies are too cowardly to harass face-to-face.

Bullies are more likely to have aggressive personalities and become easily frustrated. Their parents may not be sufficiently involved in their lives, or there may be abuse or other crises at home. Imagine how insecure and bummed these bullies are in their own skin.

Sonja has the right idea because bullies are reluctant to pick on those who project strength and self-confidence.

I see my height as a sign that I was meant to be strong in both body and mind. My tall friend gets picked on sometimes, but she always bends over to try to look smaller and always complains about her height. I never get picked on and I am almost an inch taller than she is. I am trying to help her see herself differently.

All bullies need to prop up themselves to hide their own insecurities. So, in that sense, being bullied is not even about you! You are just one tool they use to fight off their own demons.

How do you respond to these tormenters? Understanding the already warped place they are coming from should help soften the emotional pain they are trying to impose on you.

You do have choices, of course. Responding in kind is one option but be prepared for an unwelcomed uptick in intensity.

"You think I'm ugly? You apparently never looked in a mirror."

Giving back in kind may make you feel more powerful or relieve stress, but effectiveness is not guaranteed.

It may be best to stand up tall, shake your head, and just walk away. This is not a retreat. This is not cowardly. Even if they laugh or keep spewing their insults, the message has been sent that you don't care and find them unworthy of a response. (And they *are* unworthy.) Bullies don't like to be ignored because that does not fulfill their needs to make someone else feel bad.

Look at this cartoon. This is your vantage point. This nasty little person is comical. Think of this image any time a bully—boy or girl—looks up at you and tries to boost their own ego at your expense.

A word about cyberbullying: Using social media to bully involves a special type of creep who gets caught up in a mob mentality. It is difficult to respond because the bullies are not physically present and may not even be identifiable. Height alone is usually not of enough interest to bullies who want to inflict emotional pain. But it can happen. Finding emotional support is crucial. (See references about cyberbullying in the Chapter Notes for Chapter 17 at the back of the book.)

Of course, if the bullying continues and your responses have been met with mockery or an escalation, you must be more proactive. Talk to someone who is known for caring about others: a true friend, a school counselor, a religious leader, your parents or other family members, or a teacher.

CHAPTER 18

You Have a Lot in Common With Short People (Yes, Really)

If you never thought about this before, you will be surprised by how many of the challenges taller and shorter people face are similar. The world, after all, is set up for that majority in the middle.

Some of the similarities are exactly alike for both tall and short people. Others are opposite sides of the same coins.

Consider these examples:

Tall: *I get so tired of people always asking how tall I am.*
Short: *I hate it when people ask me how tall I am.*

Tall: *Do people think I am not aware of how tall I am?*
Short: *Do people really think that I don't know that I am short?*

Tall: *People always ask me to reach for things for them on the top shelves.*
Short: *People want me to get them stuff from the bottom shelf.*

Tall: *I'd rather be called "cute" than "hot."*
Short: *I'd rather be called "hot" than "cute."*

Tall: *When I am driving the sun visor blocks my view.*
Short: *When I drive, the sun visor is too high to shelter my eyes.*

Tall: *People think I am older than I am, which can cause problems when they expect me to act older.*
Short: *I get mad when people guess my age and it is three years younger than I am.*

Tall: *One-size-fits-all almost never fits me.*
Short: *One-size-fits-all rarely fits me.*

Tall: *I am always in the back row for group photos.*
Short: *I don't like to always be in the front row for group photos.*

Tall: *I have to look down on people's heads.*
Short: *I have no choice but to look up to almost everyone except children.*

Tall: *The top half of my head gets cut off in group photographs.*
Short: *The bottom half of my head gets cut off in family photos.*

Tall: *I'm always surprised when people guess my actual age.*
Short: *It makes me feel so good when people guess my age correctly.*

Tall: *Hugging most people is awkward. I have to hunch down to get my arms around their backs.*
Short: *Most people hug my head because they can't reach much lower.*

Tall: *I have trouble fitting into small cars.*
Short: *Getting into a van or truck is a chore.*

Tall: *The showerhead only comes to my neck.*
Short: *I can't reach the showerhead.*

Tall: *I have to be careful because everyone can hear me when I talk.*
Short: *I have to try to talk loud or most people can't hear me.*

Tall: *I get tired of the question, "Will you get any taller?"*
Short: *I wish people would quit asking me if I am going to get any taller.*

Tall: *My knees are crammed up under the steering wheel when I drive.*
Short: *I can hardly reach the brake and gas pedals.*

Tall: *I have to readjust everything in my car after someone else drives it.*
Short: *I have to adjust the seat, steering wheel, and mirrors back to the way they were after someone borrows my car.*

Tall: *People never let me forget how tall I am.*
Short: *People never let me forget how short I am.*

Tall: *I always have to move at a snail's pace when walking with shorter friends.*
Short: *I almost have to run when walking with my tall friend.*

Tall: *People look right up into my nose.*
Short: *Everyone can see my bad hair day.*

Tall: *People can find me whether I want them to or not.*
Short: *No one can ever find me, even when I want them to.*

So, what does it mean when people struggle with similar issues or when they are different sides of the same coin? It's time to replace any jealousy/teasing/rejecting of each other with empathy. It's always good to have solid allies with another identifiable height group. People are stronger when they are together.

CHAPTER 19

Managing the Downsides of Being a Tall Girl

This book has a single purpose—to highlight the many advantages of being a tall girl and to explore how some of the challenges can be reframed and interpreted in a more positive way. Nevertheless, not everything is in a tall girl's favor. Most every tall girl already knows that.

PRECONCEPTIONS ABOUT PEOPLE'S HEIGHT

"Heightism" is the term used to describe prejudice against people based on how tall they are.

One mostly hears about prejudice based on height as it applies to very short boys and men. But heightism can be about women as well, especially very tall women. Women above 6 feet are more likely to be the targets of ridicule and bad jokes simply because they are more visible.

INJURIES

Back problems and limb injuries are more common among tall adults. Tall girls must avoid improperly lifting heavy objects.

ERGONOMICS AND TALL PEOPLE

Ergonomics is the science of designing things to make it easy, safe, and efficient for people to use them. Every tall person knows that "people" in this case refers to those of average stature, not them!

Car seats, airplane seats, theater seats, many types of furniture and beds, bleachers, hanging light fixtures, speaker platforms, low doorways and low ceilings are examples of the plentiful evidence that tall people were not often on the minds of the designers of things.

TOO GREAT EXPECTATIONS

Sometimes tall girls feel taken advantage of. They are perceived of as being stronger and older than they are, so people may demand more of them than they can easily deliver.

Adults may say things or ask questions that are inappropriate given a tall girl's true age. Or adults may assume that a tall girl is "slow" because she does not act the age they *think* she is.

The best practice may be to just say, as one girl suggested, "I'm not older, I'm just taller."

BOYS AND TALL GIRLS

The most often discussed downside involves tall girls who want to get together with boys. Some tall young women shared that they didn't date boys until college whereas others found a boyfriend in middle school. Or tall girls didn't date in middle school or high school because they would *only* date boys taller than themselves, and there were just too few of those around.

According to some accounts, boys (including tall ones) do prefer girls shorter than themselves. It may be true that dating shorter girls makes some boys feel more in control, more "traditional," and perhaps less threatened. However, you might be surprised to learn that surveys reveal height to *not* be an issue for a sub-

stantial percentage of boys. Tall girls themselves are the ones who are more often reluctant to date shorter guys!

The good news here is that the traditional social rule that the boy should be the taller one is relaxing. Television shows more frequently portray the woman as the taller partner. In interviews with tall adult women, many found the loves of their lives to be men shorter than themselves.

But you still want a taller guy? You will run into a lot of them, but you may just have to wait until after high school or college. Puberty— that awkward period when the human body begins its transformation from girl/boy towards woman/man— starts as early as 8 and as late as 13 for girls. Those who started puberty early will have reached close to their adult height by age 13. Those who started later will keep growing up to 18. In the meantime, boys start puberty later (ages 9 to 15). It won't be until high school when boys begin to reach their adult height, and some boys will keep growing into their 20s.

Here's the best place to bring up the most difficult boy-girl interaction during the teenage years: *slow dancing*. The fit just isn't quite right, and the shorter boy's head may be where you don't want it to be. If you feel uncomfortable, politely refuse a slow dance with a much shorter guy. If he persists, gently tell him why. One tall girl I interviewed suggested that if you like the boy you could tell him that you would be happy to fast dance with him.

Now, how many tall men are there compared to women who are 5 feet 8 inches or taller? Consider the next image. As we already know, most women are shorter than most men, with the average woman standing just a smidge under 5 feet 4 inches (light gray curve). Those who stand at 5 feet 8 or taller (making up only

8% of the female population) are in the darker striped area. That is (or will be) your group. The white areas are where most of the shorter men and shorter women overlap. Now, notice how many men are 5 feet 8 to 5 feet 11 inches tall (darker gray). Lots of them. And see how many are 6 feet and taller in very dark gray. Some more!

So, never despair. Tall men are everywhere. (So are good shorter ones!)

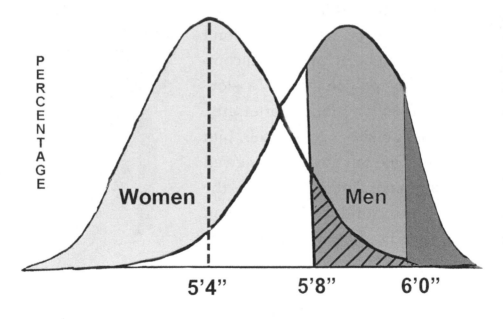

USING HEIGHT AS AN EXCUSE

You have heard this before in many contexts: "If *only* I was..." Using an excuse keeps people from solving their underlying problem.

Arista learned the hard way.

I spent so much time blaming how tall I was that I convinced myself I couldn't do anything well. I was too tall to dance. I was too tall to have a lot of friends. I was too tall to get a good job. So, I just didn't try. I even blamed my bad grades on being too tall! I finally figured out with the help of a therapist that I was withdrawn and depressed and that is why nothing was coming my way. Once I dropped my excuse, my life began to happen!

Tall girls and women often assign extra meaning to their height. So, whenever you find yourself saying, "If only I was shorter..." realize that you may have just snared yourself in your own trap.

BLOCKING OTHERS' VIEW

We usually think tall men are the ones to avoid in theaters, concerts, or parades. But every tall woman knows the soft groans from those behind her as she seats herself. Tall girls and women can only accommodate others by not wearing a high hairstyle or hat. Otherwise it is what it is. (Some tall girls say that they try to get to seated events early so they can sit in front of a seat that is still empty.)

FEELING ALONE AND DIFFERENT

We all, no matter how tall, have days when we feel lonely and isolated. Your height could be the cause of a bad day. Maybe a thoughtless schoolmate told you how glad she is to be a "normal size." The boys standing around laughed when you accidently bumped your head on the classroom airplane mobile. Or your teacher lined up everyone according to height, and you were ultimately standing alone and feeling conspicuous.

Sometimes feeling upset about being taller hangs on for a long time. This can lower self-confidence and contribute to a poor body image.

You need some caring support now! Who do you call?

Many tall girls find their support system inside their own home. One or both parents and maybe a sister or brother are also tall and understand because they are (or have been) there.

But it can happen that family members are not adequately sensitive to their tall children's concerns. Conflicts in the home diminish the ability of family members to be responsive to each other's needs.

Alternative sources of support may include involvement in a hobby group or club and having a good friend or two. A good friend is worth her weight in gold.

Tobi found an outlet.

I decided to find an activity to be excited about. I chose acting and signed up for a class. The group of interesting people also found me interesting. Even though no one else was anywhere near as tall as me, I still fit in. This has been a great boost to my self-confidence. I am in a play at my school next month. We will also perform at a children's hospital.

Isola knows the value of one good friend.

I don't have a lot of friends, but I have one who is very special. She is so easy to talk to. If I feel upset because this one irritating boy always makes a comment about my long legs, she makes me forget all about it by insisting that we go get ice cream. She always makes me laugh if I am having what I call "a bad tall day."

We all have downer days. But if you find yourself consistently depressed and need more support than is readily available, please do not resist seeking a professional counselor. There is never any shame in asking for help.

CHAPTER 20

Putting It All Together

So, where are we? We know that tall girls are rated as attractive, look more stylish in clothes, have excellent career prospects and will earn more money, are seen by others as smart and powerful, enjoy sports advantages, get noticed easily, and are remembered. No wonder most tall adult women end up being satisfied with their height! Very tall women often felt awkward and uncomfortable during adolescence, but as they grew, their height was also described as an advantage. They are happy with their stunning appearances. If given a chance to change, most would choose to remain tall. The positive impressions most others automatically have of tall people circles back and has a positive influence on how tall people see themselves.

We also know those annoying questions are often people's way of offering a compliment or of starting a conversation. Most people are impressed and assume you are proud of your tallness or they wouldn't so openly draw attention to it.

Here's some more good news. The view that petite women—short and thin—are the ultimate image of femininity is so "yesterday!" As women compete more openly and successfully in sports and high-level jobs, the concept of "an ideal-looking woman" is now varied, making plenty of space for tall, strong, active, competent women.

We know that underneath the ugly masks of teasers and bullies lie insecure losers who are desperately attempting to feel superior by making their victims feel bad. We know that tall people will endure fewer emotional assaults if they exude confidence and stand tall.

I saved for last what tall women offered when asked, "What is the best practical advice to give a tall teenage girl?" After all, they were teens once. All these women have become fulfilled, satisfied adults who are grateful for the height that helped become who they wanted to be.

Here are the top three suggestions for you to consider, in in case you haven't already.

DANCE

"Enroll in a dance class" was a frequent piece of advice. Dancing will help carry your impressive body more gracefully. Dancing builds self-confidence. It is emotionally invigorating and sets your mind free from distractions. The music that accompanies dance nourishes the soul. Those women who did not take a dance class when they were younger now regret it.

Erika's story is a common one.

Dance was my savior. It changed the way I moved. Friends noticed that I carried myself better. You don't have to be a star. You don't even have to be that good at it. I wasn't. It's all about getting out there and moving with others who are also focusing on the fun we are having.

Yvonne took an alternative route to accomplish a similar goal.

If you don't want to dance, try a modeling class. I wanted to improve my posture and my walk, even though I had

no interest in becoming a model. At first the class was weird, but the exercises were showing results. I started feeling stronger. Standing up straight with shoulders back made me feel tall and mighty.

GIVE SHORTER BOYS A CHANCE

Tall girls complain that taller boys are hard to find. (That may be true until after high school.) Is a taller boyfriend essential? Remember that studies reveal height is often less of an issue for boys than for girls. The obvious best way to increase the chances of male friendships and dating is to accept the attention of shorter guys.

Of the women who rejected boys because they were shorter, some now admit that they probably missed out on satisfactory friendships with admirable, self-confident boys while stewing over what was not available.

Janet regrets the nice boy she left in the dust.

I did not go to my high school prom. The tall boy I was attracted to chose to invite my short friend. Another boy only three inches shorter than I am did invite me, but I told him I was going out of town that weekend. I remember that he was such a nice guy who had a lot going for him. Instead I sat alone in my room on prom night, daring not to be seen and feeling ashamed for being such a snit.

Kayla's life took a joyful U turn.

At 6 feet 2 inches tall I held out for that 6-foot 3-inch guy who never materialized. Then, in college, along came Robert at 5-feet 9 inches. He would not take "no thank you" for an answer. Long story short. We are married and expecting our third child. It would take me an hour to tell you how happy I am.

FIND YOUR PASSION

The most frequent suggestion offered by tall women is, "Find what inspires you and go for it!" The teenage years are a time to explore and become absorbed with healthy, exciting activities unrelated to in-school learning. Sharing the activity with others provides social interaction and support. Or, if you prefer, your choice can be something you do on your own.

The tall women who were interviewed for this book found excitement, meaning, and dedication in many forms: acting, photography, cooking, sports, bicycling,

their church or temple, gymnastics, music, ceramics, computer programming, painting, digital graphics, and volunteering in a hospital, to name a few. All felt their involvement was a significant and positive feature of their teenage years.

Bobbi, who is 6 feet tall at age 16, is starting towards her goal early.

I have a dream. I want to be a journalist and a photographer who travels around the world creating stories about the people and places I have always wanted to visit. Italy especially. So now I practice taking photos of people and animals. I entered a photo of a cat up a tree in our county fair contest and won second prize. It's a good start.

Phyllis, age 32 at 5 feel 10 inches tall, got hooked on making jewelry when she was still in school.

I enrolled in a beading class in summer camp when I was in middle school. This class took me on a what would be a long journey I enjoy to this day. I find old broken necklaces and bracelets in second-hand shops and rework them with some new beads into modern designs. I find it so gratifying to give these discarded items a second life.

Your choice of a "passion activity" can be totally unrelated to being tall. It's coming from who you are in another way.

EXPLORING HEIGHT BEYOND THIS BOOK

Online resources allow young tall people to discover much about who they will become. Here are a few of my favorites.

The Tall Society (thetallsociety.com), as described by Founder Bree Wijnaar, is a one-of-a-kind, empowering, and inspiring community where tall girls and women worldwide unite. The community provides a welcoming sisterhood for tall women and younger tall girls who need guidance in learning how to be comfortable with their height and to love themselves. The Tall Society delivers a wide variety of content including Self-Love, Inspiration, Fashion, Life, and a video series called *Tall Talk*. Get your daily dose of inspiration, empowerment and positivity on their website and across their highly engaged social platforms.

The Tall Society also plans meet-ups worldwide called "Meet Your Tall Sisters Brunches," that provide special opportunities for our tall sisters to connect in person. The Tall Society community of "Tall Sisters" bond in a way unlike any other.

More Than My Height (morethanmyheight.com) is dedicated to enhancing confidence and tall body positivity through tips and other relatable content. Created by two beautiful tall sisters, the site offers stimulating stories. Sample article topics include a defense of dating shorter men, sports as a tall woman, lying about height, and how the media manipulates height. The founders also offer Amalli Talli, a stunning clothing line (amallitalli.com), for taller girls and women.

The Tall Life (https://tall.life) is a helpful resource, especially for physical and health related information relevant to tall men and women. Also offered are height calculators, books, and gift ideas to make tall life easier. Devices include raised cutting boards and longer camping equipment. Site founder, Sam Lochner, has a book well worth reading titled, *Tall Life*. At 6 feet 7 inches he should know!

Height Goddess (www.heightgoddess.com) Founded by a remarkable woman, Lameka Weeks, HEIGHT GODDESS started with a premise: Inspire women to love their height, embrace their uniqueness, and share their confidence and journey with others. Great podcasts offer perspectives on everything tall. Topics include defining personal excellence and growing up as a tall girl. The Facebook page is colorful and uplifting. For the self-confident girl who likes a little sass, one can purchase tee shirts with inscriptions reading, "Yes, I know I am tall," "Life is short but I'm not," "You walk, I stride," and "Sorry, not everyone can be tall."

FINAL WORDS

When you accept your height as a gift, you also make yourself a more compassionate and better person. You know what it's like to be a bit different. You can empathize with those who stand out for other reasons, sometimes in ways that make them targets for harassment or rejection. With your many advantages you can stand tall for them as well.

Bree Wijnaar, Founder of The Tall Society, created for me the perfect ending message: "Tall Sisters! Please never forget to hold your head high, keep your back straight, throw on those heels or flats and strut on! Embrace your blessing of height and lean into the power your stature brings."

Chapter Notes

Chapter 1. Introduction: Tall Girl Basics

Recommended memoir by a tall adult woman (6'3"). Arianne Cohen's *The Tall Book: A celebration of Life from on High* (2009).

Barbara Wortin's *Too Tall Alice* (2009). A cute book for young girls (8-12 yrs.) who are already very tall and expressing concerns about it.

The Law of Tall Girls (2017) by Joanne Macgregor. A good young adult novel about a tall girl and her secret.

Kid's Health. (2016). *Feeling Too Tall or Too Short*. A good overview of where height comes from. https://kidshealth.org/en/kids/my-height.html

Chapter 2. In Praise of All Things Tall

Many writings describe the world's tallest things. Here are a few examples:

Graham, I. (2012). *Megastructures: Tallest, Longest, Biggest, Deepest*.

National Geographic. (October 2009). *The Tallest Trees. Redwoods*.

Dupre, J. & Smith, A. (2013). *Updated Skyscrapers: A History of the World's Most Extraordinary Buildings*.

White, M. (2014). *Top Trails: Northern California's Redwood Coast: Must-Do Hikes for Everyone*.

Chapter 3. The Full Meaning of "Tall" in Everyday Language

Here is one example from among the hundreds of papers and books on how our words affect how we perceive reality.

Guerra, A. (2019). The power of language. The Learning Mind.
https://www.learning-mind.com/the-power-of-language/

Chapter 4. The Power of Attention

Benedictus, L. (2018). Look at me: Why attention-seeking is the
defining need of our times.
https://www.theguardian.com/society/2018/feb/05/crimes-of-
attention-stalkers-killers-jihadists-longing

Derber, C. (1979). *The Pursuit of Attention*. New York, NY: Oxford
University Press.

Wagner, P. L. (1996). *Showing Off*. Austin, TX: University of Texas
Press.

Chapter 5. Being Unforgettable

Trafton, A. (2012). How attention helps you remember. *MIT News*.
http://news.mit.edu/2012/neuroscientists-shed-light-on-plasticity-0927

Richie, J. (Jan, 2009). Fact or fiction? Elephants never forget. *Scientific American*.
https://www.scientificamerican.com/article/elephants-never-forget/

Chapter 6. You Look Great in Clothes

Simply enter "tall girl clothes" into Google for a variety of
options. It appears that every major clothing line for juniors and
women are now competing for the tall female business.

amallitalli.com/
https://teens.lovetoknow.com/Tall_Teen_Clothing
www.longtallsally.com
www.instyle.com/fashion/clothing/stores-for-tall-women

The Real Tall (http://www.therealtall.com/) offers a list of mainstream outlets that have tall clothing lines.

Elite, a top modeling agency, specifies height requirements on
its website. Women must be between 5 feet 8 inches and 5 feet 11
inches tall.
https://www.leaf.tv/articles/the-average-height-of-a-model/

The world's tallest model
http://www.guinnessworldrecords.com/world-records/tallest-professional-model

James, R. M. (Jan, 2018). What It's Like to Shop as a Tall Woman. *Racked.*
https://www.racked.com/2018/1/24/16911166/tall-woman-shopping

Opelka, B. (April, 2018). 9 fashion struggles that every tall person can relate to. *Insider.*
www.thisisinsider.com/tall-clothes-shopping-problems-tips-2018-3

Chapter 7. Oh, Those Legs!

Sample, I. (Jan, 2008). Why men and women find longer legs more attractive. *The Guardian.*
www.theguardian.com/science/2008/jan/17/humanbehaviour.psychology

Louise, C. (April 2016). Why do models have to be tall? *The Guardian.*
https://www.ukmodels.co.uk/library/why-do-models-have-to-be-tall/

Chapter 8. You Don't Have to Wear Heels (Unless You Want to)

Here are just a few of the available resources about the dangers of high heel shoes and how to minimize them.

Caba, J. (July 7, 2015). Negative effects of high heels: New research confirms what wearing high heels can do to women's ankles, *Medical Daily.*
https://www.medicaldaily.com/negative-effects-high-heels-new-research-confirms-what-wearing-high-heels-can-do-341594

Renee, A. (2018) 10 reasons you should not wear high heels anymore. *Consumer Health Digest.*
https://www.consumerhealthdigest.com/general-health/10-reasons-you-should-not-wear-high-heels.html

Reynolds, G. (Jan. 25, 2012). A scientific look at the dangers of high heels. *New York Times.*
https://well.blogs.nytimes.com/2012/01/25/scientists-look-at-the-dangers-of-high-heels/

Wikihow Staff. (no date) How to be comfortable wearing high heels when you're tall
https://www.wikihow.com/Be-Comfortable-Wearing-High-Heels-when-You%27re-Tall

And an article defending tall women wearing high heels.
Komar, M. (2016). 21 Tall women wearing heels because being "too tall" isn't a thing.
https://www.bustle.com/articles/146638-21-tall-women-wearing-heels-because-being-too-tall-isnt-a-thing-photos

Chapter 9. Teenagers' Obsession with Dieting—Probably Not Your Problem!

Gavin, M. L. (2019). The deal with diets (for teens).
https://kidshealth.org/en/teens/dieting.html

National Institutes of Health. Dieting: information for teens. (2004).
https://www.ncbi.nlm.nih.gov/pmc/articles/PMC2720872/

National Institutes of Health. Adolescent dieting. (2004).
https://www.ncbi.nlm.nih.gov/pmc/articles/PMC2720870/

Chapter 10. Those Annoying Questions Are (Usually) Compliments

Hyland, C. Y. (2015). 10 questions tall people get asked every day. *Odyssey*.
https://www.theodysseyonline.com/10-things-tall-people-asked-every-day

Grebey, J. (2014). 17 questions you shouldn't ask a tall person. *BuzzFeed*.
https://www.buzzfeed.com/jamesgrebey/questions-tall-people-are-sick-of-being-asked

Chapter 11. The Sporting Edge

An article in *The Sportster* featured women athletes who are at least 6 feet tall. Aside from their exceptional successes in sports, each one is gorgeous. Check out the examples given in Chapter 11 here:

https://www.thesportster.com/entertainment/glamazons-top-15-steamiest-female-athletes-over-6-feet-tall/

Amazing women's basketball team in the 2016 Olympics
www.usab.com/history/national-team-womens/woly-2016.aspx

Peterson, D. (2009). Taller athletes are faster. *Live Science.*
www.livescience.com/7819-taller-athletes-faster-study-finds.html

Parker, K. T. (2017). *Strong is the New Pretty.* Parker Photography, Inc.
(Highly recommended book for teenage girls. Very empowering.)

Chapter 12. Tall and Smart

Case, A., & Paxson, C. (2006). Stature and status: height, ability, and labor market outcomes. *National Bureau of Economic Research.*
https://www.nber.org/papers/w12466

Yirka, B. (2014). Study finds genetic link between height and IQ. *Medicalxpress.*
https://m.medicalxpress.com/news/2014-03-genetic-link-height-iq.html

Chapter 13. Tall on the Job

Feintzeig, R. (June 9, 2014). Want to be CEO? Stand Tall. *Wall Street Journal.*
https://blogs.wsj.com/atwork/2014/06/09/tall-ceos-how-height-helps/

Nancy M. Blaker, N., Rompa, I, et al (2013). The height leadership advantage in men and women: Testing evolutionary psychology predictions about the perceptions of tall leaders. *Group Processes & Intergroup Relations,* pp. 17-27.

Dittman, M. (2004). Standing tall pays off, study finds. *Monitor on Psychology,* American Psychological Association.
https://www.apa.org/monitor/julaug04/standing

Fry, M. (2013). View from the top: Does height help business-women? Experts offer their take.
https://njbiz.com/view-from-the-top-does-height-help-business-women-experts-offer-their-take/

Career Bliss Team. (2013). Are taller women more successful at work? www.careerbliss.com/advice/are-taller-women-more-successful-at-work/

Lebowitz, S. (2015). Science says being tall could make you richer and more successful- here's why. *Business Insider US*. www.businessinsider.my/tall-people-are-richer-and-successful-2015-9/

Psychology Today Staff (2003). Tall People Get Paid More: Tall people enjoy a lifelong advantage. Companies reward stature with a larger paycheck. www.psychologytoday.com/us/articles/200310/tall-people-get-paid-more

Pinsker, J. (2015). The financial perks of being tall. https://www.theatlantic.com/business/archive/2015/05/the-financial-perks-of-being-tall/393518/

Judge, A. T. & Cable, D. M. (2004). The effect of physical height on workplace success and income: preliminary test of a theoretical model. *Journal of Applied Psychology*.

Daily Mail Reporter (2010). Tall women's salaries leave short girls in the shade. https://www.dailymail.co.uk/news/article-1265300/Tall-womens-salaries-leave-short-girls-shade.html

Donohue, M. (2007). Why tall people make more money. CNN. www.cnn.com/2007/US/Careers/02/02/cb.tall.people/index.html

LaFave, D., & Thomas, D. (May 2016). Height and cognition at work: labor market productivity in a low income setting. *Development Economics, Labor Studies*. https://www.nber.org/papers/w22290

Martin, S. W. (2019). A salesperson's ideal height and do tall salespeople sell more? https://heavyhittersales.typepad.com/heavy_hitter_sales_sales_/2017/03/a-salespersons-ideal-height-and-do-tall-salespeople-sell-more.html

Chapter 14. Unkind Jokes—Tall People Don't Have It as Bad

Books filled with dumb, stupid humor are popular, and no one escapes being a target. Just two from hundreds of examples are *The Dumb Book: Silly Stories, Stupid People*, and *Mega Mistakes that Crack Us Up*, both compiled by the editors of *The Reader's Digest*.

Chapter 15. Finding Each Other

Origins of the term, "birds of a feather..."
https://en.wiktionary.org/wiki/birds_of_a_feather_flock_together

Swami, V. (2017). Why opposites rarely attract.
https://theconversation.com/why-opposites-rarely-attract-74873

Chapter 16. Four Great Perks: Running, Reaching, Standing Above the Crowd, and the Passenger Seat

Whaley, A. (no date). Live strong. Does height matter in running?
www.livestrong.com/article/472824-does-height-matter-in-running/

Chapter 17. Looking Down on Teasers and Bullies (and What Else You Need to Know About Them)

Robinson, L. & Segal, J. (2018). *Help Guide. Bullying and cyberbullying.*
https://www.helpguide.org/articles/abuse/bullying-and-cyberbul-lying.htm/ (Excellent resource)

Englander, E. K. (2013). *Bullying and Cyberbullying: What Every Educator Needs to Know.*
https://www.amazon.com/Bullying-Cyberbullying-Every-Educator-Needs/dp/1612505996

Hinduja, S. & Patchin, J. W. (2014). *Bullying Beyond the Schoolyard: Preventing and Responding to Cyberbullying.*
https://www.amazon.com/Bullying-Beyond-Schoolyard-Preventing-Cyberbullying/dp/1483349934/ref=dp_ob_image_bk

U.S. Department of Health and Human Services. *Stop Bullying.*
https://www.stopbullying.gov/
This useful site includes details on cyberbullying and tactics, who is at risk for school bullying, what parents and teachers can do,

and many more useful topics. There are three types of bullying, according to the government's *Stop Bullying* program: (1) those who make verbal comments such as teasing, calling names, or making threats; (2) those who make social attacks such as leaving someone out, telling others to not be friends with the target, spreading rumors, or posting negative comments or photos on social media; and (3) those who physically attack, such as hitting, tripping, or taking the target's property.

Chapter 18. You Have a Lot in Common With Short People (Yes, Really)

Stryker, S. (no date or title).
www.buzzfeed.com/leonoraepstein/short-people-vs-tall-people.
(Amusing contrast of short and tall people issues)

Chapter 19. Managing the Downsides of Being a Tall Girl

Lochner, S. (2016). *Tall life*. The author, a mechanical engineer who stands 6'7", details spinal and other health and issues as they relate to being tall.

Jean-Baptiste, L. (2018). Height shaming: Tall women tell us their experiences.
https://www.refinery29.com/en-gb/height-shaming

Black, A. (2018). In defense of dating shorter men.
https://morethanmyheight.com/2018/07/19/in-defense-of-dating-shorter-men/

Chapter 20. Putting It All Together

Rosenthal, A. (2018). 7 Ways how being tall has made me a better person.
https://morethanmyheight.com/2018/09/20/7-ways-that-being-a-tall-girl-has-made-me-a-better-person/

Elizabeth, R. (no date). Too tall to date. Few men meet *our* own height requirements .
https://www.match.com/magazine/article/6563/Too-Tall-To-Date/
(Insightful personal comments about the author's "height restrictions")

Business Insider (2013). 11 Male Celebrities who are in relationships with taller women.
www.businessinsider.com/male-celebrities-with-taller-women-2013-1

TallWomen.Org. Famous tall ladies.
https://www.tallwomen.org/tall-women-stuff/famous-tall-ladies/
(Excellent collection of outstanding female role models who are also tall)

Casano, A. (no date). Famous women who are way taller than you already thought. *Ranker*.
https://www.ranker.com/list/tall-famous-women/anncasano

J. Lever, D. A. Frederick et al. (2007). Tall women's satisfaction with their height: General population data challenge assumptions behind medical interventions to stunt girls' growth. *Journal of Adolescent Health*, 40, 192-194.

Recommended Websites:

The Tall Society https://thetallsociety.com/
More Than My Height https://morethanmyheight.com/
Height Goddess https://www.heightgoddess.com/
Tall Life https://tall.life/

About the Author

Patricia Keith-Spiegel's interest in the effects of early experience on children's later development along with having tall members in her family inspired her to write *Awesome Advantages of Being a Tall Girl*. She earned her Doctor of Philosophy degree in general psychology, focusing on child development and ethical practices. She is Professor Emerita of Psychology at California State University Northridge and the Voran Honors Distinguished Professor of Psychological Science Emerita at Ball State University. As a Visiting Professor at Harvard Medical School, Department of Psychiatry at Children's Hospital, she and her colleagues conducted a research grant project supported by the National Institutes of Mental Health. She is a recipient of the Distinguished Professor Award, bestowed by the American Psychological Foundation. Patricia currently lives with her husband and dog Buzz in Walnut Creek, California. This is her 13th book.

Made in the USA
Coppell, TX
25 August 2021